S0-ABV-637

Contents

20

32

60

Main Entrées

Savory Garlic Steak with Charred Tomato Salsa

PREP TIME: 15 minutes   **MARINATE TIME:** 30 minutes
COOK TIME: 10 minutes

- ½ cup Lawry's® Italian Garlic Steak Marinade With Roasted Garlic & Olive Oil
- 1 lb. boneless flank steak
- 1½ tsp. Lawry's® Garlic Salt
- 1 medium onion, cut into ½-inch rings
- 1½ lbs. whole vine ripened tomatoes
- 2 Tbsp. chopped fresh cilantro
- 2 Tbsp. lime juice
- 1 chipotle chili in adobo sauce, finely chopped

1. In large resealable plastic bag, pour Lawry's® Italian Garlic Steak Marinade With Roasted Garlic & Olive Oil over steak; turn to coat. Close bag and marinate in refrigerator 30 minutes.

2. Remove steak from Marinade, discarding Marinade. Grill or broil steak, turning once, 8 minutes or until desired doneness. Remove and keep warm.

3. Meanwhile, evenly sprinkle ½ teaspoon Lawry's® Garlic Salt on onion. Grill or broil onion and tomatoes, turning once, 10 minutes or until browned. Chop tomatoes and onion; stir in remaining ingredients. Serve with grilled steak.

4 servings

Grilled Steak and Peppers with Chile Lime Sauce

PREP TIME: 10 minutes   **MARINATE TIME:** 30 minutes
COOK TIME: 15 minutes

1	cup Lawry's® Mexican Chile & Lime Marinade With Lime Juice
1½	lbs. boneless sirloin, skirt or flank steak
¼	cup Hellmann's® or Best Foods® Real Mayonnaise
¼	cup sour cream
¼	tsp. Lawry's® Garlic Salt
3	red, yellow and/or green bell peppers, quartered

1. In large resealable plastic bag, pour ½ cup Lawry's® Mexican Chile & Lime Marinade With Lime Juice over steak. Close bag and marinate in refrigerator 30 minutes.

2. In small bowl combine Mayonnaise, sour cream and Lawry's® Garlic Salt. Set aside.

3. Remove steak from Marinade, discarding Marinade. Grill steak and peppers, turning once and brushing with remaining ½ cup Marinade, to desired doneness. Let steak stand covered 10 minutes before slicing. Serve with mayonnaise mixture.

6 servings

*Also terrific with **Lawry's® Steak & Chop Marinade With Garlic & Cracked Black Pepper** or **Lawry's® Mesquite Marinade With Lime Juice.***

Mesquite Grilled Steak

PREP TIME: 10 minutes   **MARINATE TIME:** 30 minutes
COOK TIME: 20 minutes

1   **cup Lawry's® Mesquite Marinade With Lime Juice**
1½   **lb. steak, 1-inch thick**

1. In resealable plastic bag, pour Lawry's® Mesquite Marinade With Lime Juice over steak; turn to coat.

2. Close bag and marinate in refrigerator 30 minutes.

3. Remove steak from Marinade, discarding Marinade. Grill or broil steak to desired doneness, brushing, if desired, with additional Marinade.

4 servings

Pineapple Teriyaki Chicken Kabobs

PREP TIME: 15 minutes   **MARINATE TIME:** 30 minutes
COOK TIME: 15 minutes

- ¾ cup Lawry's® Teriyaki Marinade With Pineapple Juice
- 1 can (20 oz.) pineapple chunks in natural juice, drained (reserve 2 Tbsp. juice)
- 1 tsp. Dijon mustard
- 1 lb. boneless, skinless chicken breasts, cut into 1-inch pieces
- 2 medium red or green bell peppers, cut into 1-inch pieces
- 1 medium zucchini, cut into 1-inch pieces

1. In large resealable plastic bag, combine Lawry's® Teriyaki Marinade With Pineapple Juice, reserved pineapple juice and mustard. Add chicken; toss to coat. Close bag and marinate in refrigerator 30 minutes.

2. Remove chicken from marinade, discarding marinade. Alternately thread chicken and remaining ingredients onto skewers.* Grill or broil, turning occasionally and brushing with remaining ¼ cup marinade, 10 minutes or until chicken is thoroughly cooked.

4 servings

If using wooden skewers, soak in water at least 30 minutes prior to use.

VARIATION: *For Pineapple & Shrimp Teriyaki Kabobs, substitute shrimp for chicken and use bell peppers and red onion.*

Grilled White Pizza

PREP TIME: 15 minutes   **MARINATE TIME:** 30 minutes
COOK TIME: 13 minutes

- ½ cup PLUS 1 Tbsp. Lawry's® Mexican Chile & Lime Marinade With Lime Juice
- ½ lb. boneless, skinless chicken breasts
- 1 medium green bell pepper, quartered
- 1 medium red onion, cut into ½-inch thick slices
- ¼ cup sour cream
- 1 (12-inch) prebaked pizza crust
- 1 cup crumbled queso fresco or shredded Monterey Jack cheese (about 4 oz.)

1. In large resealable plastic bag, pour ¼ cup Lawry's® Mexican Chile & Lime Marinade With Lime Juice over chicken; turn to coat. In another resealable plastic bag, pour ¼ cup Marinade over vegetables; turn to coat. Close bags and marinate in refrigerator 30 minutes.

2. Meanwhile, in small bowl, combine sour cream with remaining 1 tablespoon Marinade; set aside.

3. Remove chicken and vegetables from Marinades, discarding Marinades. Grill chicken and vegetables, turning once, 8 minutes or until chicken is thoroughly cooked and vegetables are tender. Wrap pepper in aluminum foil; let stand 5 minutes, then remove skin and thinly slice. Thinly slice chicken.

4. Grill pizza crust 1 minute; remove from grill. Evenly spread crust with sour cream mixture, then top with chicken, vegetables and cheese. Grill covered 3 minutes or until cheese is melted.

4 servings

Also terrific with **Lawry's® Mesquite Marinade With Lime Juice, Lawry's® Steak & Chop Marinade With Garlic & Cracked Black Pepper** *or* **Lawry's® Baja Chipotle Marinade With Lime Juice.**

Apple Chicken on a Can

PREP TIME: 10 minutes   COOK TIME: 1 hour 20 minutes

4   lb. roasting chicken
1   can (14.5 oz.) chicken broth
1   cup apple cider or apple juice
3   Tbsp. Lawry's® Dijon & Honey Marinade
     With Lemon Juice
2   tsp. Lawry's® Seasoned Salt
½   tsp. Lawry's® Seasoned Pepper

1. Remove broth from can; set aside broth. Remove label from can and wash well. In can, combine apple cider with Lawry's® Dijon & Honey Marinade With Lemon Juice; set aside.

2. Sprinkle chicken with Lawry's® Seasoned Salt and Seasoned Pepper. In roasting pan, stand chicken up, inserting filled can into the cavity. Pour 1 cup broth into pan and cover tightly with aluminum foil. Grill, rotating pan occasionally, 1 hour 20 minutes or until thermometer inserted in thickest part reaches 165°F. Carefully remove can from chicken, pouring broth mixture into pan. Remove chicken to cutting board; discard can.

3. Cook broth mixture over medium-high heat, scraping up brown bits from bottom. Simmer, stirring occasionally, 8 minutes.

8 servings

TIP: *Remove foil during last 10 minutes of cooking to brown chicken. For a thicker gravy, stir 2 tablespoons all-purpose flour into ¼ cup broth or water until smooth. Stir into gravy. Bring to a boil, then simmer, stirring frequently, 8 minutes or until thickened.*

Lawry's® Grilled Maple Country-Style Ribs

PREP TIME: 15 minutes   **COOK TIME:** 2 hours

2½	to 3 lbs. country style pork ribs
1½	tsp. Lawry's® Seasoned Salt
1½	tsp. Lawry's® Garlic Salt
¾	cup pure maple syrup
¾	cup ketchup
2	Tbsp. Worcestershire sauce
1	Tbsp. prepared yellow mustard
1	tsp. hot pepper sauce

1. Preheat oven to 325°F. In 13×9-inch baking dish arrange ribs. Season with 1 teaspoon each Lawry's® Seasoned Salt and Garlic Salt; set aside.

2. In medium bowl, combine remaining ingredients. Evenly spoon ½ cup sauce over ribs. Bake covered 2 hours or until ribs are tender; drain.

3. Grill ribs, turning occasionally and brushing with remaining sauce, 10 minutes or until browned.

4 servings

TIP: *Try this sauce on chicken wings for a great party appetizer.*

Skewered Grilled Jambalaya Salad

PREP TIME: 40 minutes   **MARINATE TIME:** 30 minutes
COOK TIME: 10 minutes

½	**lb. boneless, skinless chicken breasts, cut into bite-size pieces**
½	**lb. uncooked medium shrimp, peeled and deveined**
4	**ounces andouille sausage, cut into 1-inch pieces**
½	**lb. okra, trimmed and halved**
2	**medium red bell peppers, cut into 1-inch pieces**
1	**medium onion, cut into 1-inch pieces**
½	**cup Lawry's® Caribbean Jerk Marinade With Papaya Juice**
¼	**cup Bertolli® Classico™ Olive Oil**
1	**tsp. cayenne pepper sauce**
2	**Tbsp. water**
8	**cups torn romaine lettuce leaves**
1	**cup cherry tomatoes**

1. On skewers,* alternately thread chicken, shrimp, sausage, okra, red pepper and onion. In 13×9-inch glass baking dish, pour ¼ cup Lawry's® Caribbean Jerk Marinade With Papaya Juice over skewers; turn to coat. Cover; refrigerate 30 minutes.

2. In small bowl, combine remaining ¼ cup Marinade, Olive Oil, cayenne pepper sauce and water; set aside.

3. Remove skewers from Marinade, discarding Marinade. Grill or broil skewers, turning once, 8 minutes or until chicken is thoroughly cooked and shrimp turn pink.

4. On large platter, arrange lettuce and cherry tomatoes. Top with skewers and drizzle with marinade dressing.

6 servings

* If using wooden skewers, soak at least 30 minutes.

Also terrific with **Lawry's® Hawaiian Marinade With Tropical Fruit Juices.**

Pork Chops
with Cranberry-Jalapeño Relish

PREP TIME: 25 minutes   **MARINATE TIME:** 30 minutes
COOK TIME: 15 minutes

- ½ **cup PLUS 2 Tbsp. Lawry's® Hawaiian Marinade With Tropical Fruit Juices**
- 4 **bone-in pork chops, about 1-inch thick (about 2 lbs.)**
- 2 **medium red, orange, yellow and/or green bell peppers, diced**
- 2 **jalapeño peppers, seeded and diced**
- 1 **medium cucumber, seeded and diced**
- ½ **large red onion, diced**
- ½ **cup chopped dried cranberries or apricots**
- ¼ **tsp. Lawry's® Garlic Salt**

1. In large resealable plastic bag, pour ½ cup Lawry's® Hawaiian Marinade With Tropical Fruit Juices over chops; turn to coat. Close bag and marinate in refrigerator 30 minutes.

2. In medium bowl, combine 2 tablespoons Marinade with remaining ingredients.

3. Remove chops from Marinade, discarding Marinade. Grill chops, turning once, 15 minutes or until chops are done. To serve, arrange chops on serving platter and top with relish.

4 servings

*Also terrific with **Lawry's® Caribbean Jerk Marinade With Papaya Juice**.*

Mesquite Grilled Stuffed Peppers

PREP TIME: 30 minutes   **COOK TIME:** 40 minutes

- ¾ **cup Lawry's® Mesquite Marinade With Lime Juice**
- ½ **tsp. crushed red pepper flakes**
- ½ **cup regular or converted rice**
- 6 **medium red and/or yellow bell peppers**
- 1 **medium onion, cut into ½-inch thick slices**
- 1 **can (15.5 oz.) black beans, rinsed and drained**
- 1 **can (14.5 oz.) diced tomatoes, drained**
- 2 **cups shredded cheddar cheese (about 8 oz.)**

1. In small bowl, combine Lawry's® Mesquite Marinade With Lime Juice and crushed red pepper flakes. In 2-quart saucepan, cook rice according to package directions, adding ¼ cup marinade mixture.

2. Meanwhile, grill red peppers and onion, turning occasionally and brushing with remaining marinade mixture, 10 minutes or until peppers and onion are tender. Carefully cut peppers in half, remove seeds and stem, then drain on paper towels; chop onion.

3. In large bowl, combine onion, rice, beans, tomatoes and 1 cup cheese; evenly fill peppers with rice mixture.

4. On cookie sheet, arrange 18×20-inch piece heavy-duty aluminum foil. Arrange peppers in center of foil, then top with remaining cheese. Spray another 18×20-inch piece heavy-duty aluminum foil with nonstick cooking spray, then place sprayed-side-down on peppers. Seal foil edges airtight with double fold. Gently slide pouch off cookie sheet onto grill. Grill 10 minutes or until cheese is melted and peppers are heated through.

4 servings

Grilled Eggplant Parmesan

PREP TIME: 15 minutes   **MARINATE TIME:** 15 minutes
COOK TIME: 15 minutes

¾	cup Lawry's® Italian Garlic Steak Marinade With Roasted Garlic & Olive Oil
1	medium eggplant, cut into ½-inch thick slices
1	medium tomato, sliced
1½	cups shredded fresh mozzarella cheese (about 6 oz.)
¼	tsp. Lawry's® Seasoned Pepper
¼	cup fresh basil leaves (optional)

1. In large resealable plastic bag, pour ½ cup Lawry's® Italian Garlic Steak Marinade With Roasted Garlic & Olive Oil over eggplant; turn to coat. Close bag and marinate 15 minutes.

2. Remove eggplant from Marinade. Grill, turning once and brushing with remaining ¼ cup Marinade, 10 minutes or until tender.

3. Top grilled eggplant with tomato, mozzarella and Lawry's® Seasoned Pepper. Grill 2 minutes or until cheese is melted. Garnish with basil, if desired.

4 servings

*Also terrific with **Lawry's® Herb & Garlic Marinade With Lemon Juice.***

TIP: *Serve on a grilled hamburger bun for an easy and quick sandwich.*

Chile Lime Fish Tacos

PREP TIME: 10 minutes **MARINATE TIME:** 15 minutes
COOK TIME: 8 minutes

- ¾ **cup Lawry's® Mexican Chile & Lime Marinade With Lime Juice**
- 1 **lb. tilapia fillets**
- ½ **cup sour cream**
- 1 **medium ripe avocado**
- ½ **tsp. Lawry's® Garlic Salt**
- 8 **corn tortillas**

1. In large resealable plastic bag, pour ½ cup Lawry's® Mexican Chile & Lime Marinade With Lime Juice over fillets. Close bag and marinate in refrigerator 15 minutes.

2. Meanwhile, in small bowl combine sour cream and 2 tablespoons Marinade. In another bowl, mash avocado with Lawry's® Garlic Salt; cover. Chill until ready to serve.

3. Remove fillets from Marinade, discarding Marinade. Grill, turning once and brushing with remaining 2 tablespoons Marinade 6 minutes or until fillets flake with a fork.

4. To serve, evenly spread avocado mixture on tortillas, then top with crumbled fillets and sour cream mixture. Garnish, if desired, with salsa, shredded Mexican blend cheese and/or shredded cabbage.

4 servings

*Also terrific with **Lawry's® Baja Chipotle Marinade With Lime Juice.***

Sesame Salmon on a Raft with Grilled Vegetables

PREP TIME: 15 minutes **MARINATE TIME:** 30 minutes
COOK TIME: 15 minutes

¾	cup Lawry's® Sesame Ginger Marinade With Mandarin Orange Juice
2½	lb. salmon fillet
	Cedar plank
¼	cup sliced green onions
1	Tbsp. sesame seeds
1	tsp. Lawry's® Garlic Salt
3	medium red, yellow and/or orange bell peppers, quartered
2	large onions, sliced into thick rounds
2	medium zucchini, cut into ⅜-inch thick diagonal slices
2	Tbsp. Bertolli® Classico™ Olive Oil

1. In large resealable plastic bag, pour Lawry's® Sesame Ginger Marinade With Mandarin Orange Juice over salmon; turn to coat. Close bag and marinate in refrigerator 30 minutes.

2. Grill cedar plank* 5 minutes; remove from grill. Remove salmon from Marinade, discarding Marinade. On charred side of cedar plank, arrange salmon skin-side-down. On cedar plank, grill salmon, covered, 10 minutes or until salmon flakes with a fork. Sprinkle with green onions and sesame seeds.

3. Meanwhile, in large bowl, toss vegetables with Olive Oil. Grill, turning once, 4 minutes or until vegetables are golden and tender; cut peppers. Serve grilled vegetables with salmon.

10 servings

Soak cedar plank in water at least 4 hours prior to grilling.

Shrimp Salad Delight

PREP TIME: 15 minutes   **MARINATE TIME:** 30 minutes
COOK TIME: 10 minutes

½   cup Lawry's® Lemon Pepper Marinade With
      Lemon Juice

¼   tsp. Lawry's® Garlic Salt

1   lb. uncooked large shrimp, peeled and deveined
      with tails on

2   medium green, red and/or yellow bell peppers,
      sliced

1   cup sliced onion

¼   tsp. Lawry's® Seasoned Salt

¼   tsp. Lawry's® Seasoned Pepper

1   Tbsp. Shedd's Spread Country Crock® Spread

1   cup halved cherry or grape tomatoes

1   package (8 oz.) spring salad mix

¼   cup shredded pepper Jack cheese (about 1 oz.)

1. In large resealable plastic bag, combine Lawry's® Lemon Pepper Marinade With Lemon Juice, Garlic Salt and shrimp; turn to coat. Close bag and marinate in refrigerator 30 minutes.

2. Meanwhile, in center of double layer (12×18-inch pieces) heavy-duty aluminum foil, arrange peppers and onion. Top with Lawry's® Seasoned Salt, Seasoned Pepper and Spread. Wrap foil loosely around vegetables, sealing edges airtight with double fold. Grill 10 minutes or until vegetables are tender.

3. Remove shrimp from marinade, discarding marinade. Grill or broil shrimp, turning once, until shrimp turn pink.

4. In large bowl, toss vegetables with their juices, shrimp and tomatoes. On serving platter, arrange spring mix. Top with shrimp mixture. Sprinkle with cheese.

4 servings

Chopped Mexican Salad

PREP TIME: 30 minutes   **MARINATE TIME:** 30 minutes
COOK TIME: 10 minutes

- ¾ cup Lawry's® Mexican Chile & Lime Marinade With Lime Juice
- 1 lb. boneless, skinless chicken breasts
- 1 medium red onion, cut into ½-inch slices
- 1 medium green bell pepper, cored and quartered
- 1 cup sour cream
- 2 Tbsp. milk
- 1 Tbsp. chopped fresh cilantro
- 8 cups torn romaine or iceberg lettuce leaves
- 1 cup frozen, thawed or drained canned whole kernel corn
- 1 cup chickpeas or garbanzos, rinsed and drained
- 1 medium tomato, halved horizontally and seeded
- 1 medium avocado, diced
- ½ cup crumbled queso fresco cheese or Monterey Jack cheese (about 2 oz.)
- 1 cup crushed plain tortilla chips

1. In 2 separate resealable plastic bags, pour ¼ cup Lawry's® Mexican Chile & Lime Marinade With Lime Juice over chicken, then ¼ cup Marinade over onion and green pepper; turn to coat. Close bags and marinate in refrigerator 30 minutes.

2. Meanwhile, in medium bowl, blend sour cream, milk, cilantro and remaining ¼ cup Marinade until smooth; chill, if desired.

3. Remove chicken and vegetables from Marinade, discarding Marinade. Grill chicken and vegetables, turning once, 10 minutes or until chicken is thoroughly cooked and vegetables are tender. Thinly slice chicken, then chop onion and green pepper.

4. On serving platter, arrange lettuce. Top with chicken, green pepper, corn, chickpeas, tomato and avocado. Evenly top with cheese and tortilla chips, then serve with sour cream mixture.

4 servings

*Also terrific with **Lawry's**® **Mesquite Marinade With Lime Juice** or **Lawry's**® **Baja Chipotle Marinade With Lime Juice**.*

Dijon & Honey Grilled Cobb Salad

PREP TIME: 20 minutes   **MARINATE TIME:** 30 minutes
COOK TIME: 10 minutes

- ¼ cup PLUS 2 Tbsp. Lawry's® Dijon & Honey Marinade With Lemon Juice
- 1 lb. boneless, skinless chicken breasts
- ½ cup Hellmann's® or Best Foods® Real Mayonnaise
- 8 cups coarsely chopped iceberg or romaine lettuce leaves
- 8 slices bacon, crisp-cooked and crumbled
- 1 cup canned black beans, rinsed and drained
- 1 cup frozen, thawed or drained canned whole kernel corn
- 1 medium tomato, chopped
- 1 cup shredded cheddar cheese (about 4 oz.)
  Candied Pecans*

1. In large resealable plastic bag, pour ¼ cup Lawry's® Dijon & Honey Marinade With Lemon Juice over chicken; turn to coat. Close bag and marinate in refrigerator 30 minutes.

2. Meanwhile, in small bowl, combine Mayonnaise and remaining 2 tablespoons Marinade; set aside.

3. Remove chicken from Marinade, discarding Marinade. Grill chicken, turning once, 10 minutes or until chicken is thoroughly cooked; thinly slice.

4. On large serving platter, arrange lettuce. Top with chicken, bacon, beans, corn, tomato and cheese; arranging in rows. Just before serving, sprinkle with candied pecans. Serve with mayonnaise mixture.

4 servings

For Candied Pecans, in 12-inch nonstick skillet, cook 1 cup chopped pecans, ⅓ cup sugar and ½ teaspoon Lawry's® Seasoned Salt over medium heat, stirring frequently, 10 minutes or until sugar browns. Spread pecan mixture onto greased aluminum foil. Let cool. Break into bite-size pieces.

Burgers, Sandwiches & Snacks

Stuffed Southwest Burgers

PREP TIME: 20 minutes   **COOK TIME:** 10 minutes

- ½ cup PLUS 2 Tbsp. Lawry's® Baja Chipotle Marinade With Lime Juice
- ¼ cup Hellmann's® or Best Foods® Real Mayonnaise
- 1 tsp. Lawry's® Seasoned Salt
- 1 lb. ground beef
- 1 cup shredded pepper Jack cheese (about 4 oz.)
- 1 medium onion, cut into 4 slices
- 4 hamburger buns, toasted
- 1 avocado, sliced

1. In small bowl, combine ¼ cup Marinade and ¼ cup Mayonnaise; set aside.

2. In large bowl, combine ¼ cup Lawry's® Baja Chipotle Marinade With Lime Juice, Seasoned Salt and ground beef; shape into 8 patties. Evenly arrange cheese on center of 4 patties. Top with remaining patties; seal edges tight. Grill, turning once, 10 minutes or until desired doneness.

3. Meanwhile, grill onion, turning once and brushing with remaining 2 tablespoons Marinade, 10 minutes or until tender.

4. To serve, spread mayonnaise mixture on buns, then top with burgers, onion, avocado and, if desired, lettuce and tomato.

4 servings

Portobello Mushroom Burgers

PREP TIME: 10 minutes   **MARINATE TIME:** 15 minutes
COOK TIME: 15 minutes

- **1 cup PLUS 1 Tbsp. Lawry's® Italian Garlic Steak Marinade With Roasted Garlic & Olive Oil**
- **4 medium portobello mushrooms, cleaned and stems removed**
- **¼ cup Hellmann's® or Best Foods® Real Mayonnaise**
- **¼ tsp. Lawry's® Seasoned Pepper**
- **4 slices provolone cheese (about 4 oz.)**
- **4 Kaiser rolls**
- **1 jar (7 oz.) roasted red peppers, drained and sliced**
- **1 cup arugula or baby spinach leaves**

1. In large resealable plastic bag, pour 1 cup Lawry's® Italian Garlic Steak Marinade With Roasted Garlic & Olive Oil over mushrooms; turn to coat. Close bag and marinate 15 minutes.

2. In small bowl, combine Mayonnaise, remaining 1 tablespoon Marinade and Lawry's® Seasoned Pepper; set aside.

3. Remove mushrooms from Marinade, reserving Marinade. Grill mushrooms, turning occasionally and brushing with reserved marinade, 15 minutes or until tender. Top with cheese and cook until cheese is melted.

4. On rolls, evenly spread mayonnaise mixture, then toast on grill. To serve, top rolls with burger, roasted pepper and arugula.

4 servings

*Also terrific with **Lawry's® Herb & Garlic Marinade With Lemon Juice.***

Sautéed Onion & Bacon Cheeseburger Deluxe

PREP TIME: 15 minutes   **COOK TIME:** 10 minutes

4	slices bacon, chopped
1	medium onion, sliced
½	cup shredded Mexican blend cheese (about 2 oz.)
½	cup Lawry's® Steak & Chop Marinade With Garlic & Cracked Black Pepper
¼	tsp. Lawry's® Seasoned Salt
¼	tsp. Lawry's® Seasoned Pepper
1	lb. ground beef
4	hamburger buns, toasted if desired
¼	cup Hellmann's® or Best Foods® Real Mayonnaise

1. In 10-inch nonstick skillet, cook bacon over medium heat, stirring occasionally, 5 minutes or until crisp. Remove bacon and drain on paper towels; reserve 1 tablespoon drippings.

2. In reserved drippings, cook onion over medium heat, stirring occasionally until tender. Remove skillet from heat. Stir in bacon, cheese and 2 tablespoons Lawry's® Steak & Chop Marinade With Garlic & Cracked Black Pepper; set aside.

3. In medium bowl, combine Lawry's® Seasoned Salt, Seasoned Pepper and ground beef; shape into 4 patties.

4. Grill or broil hamburgers, turning once and brushing with remaining Marinade, to desired doneness. Evenly spread buns with Mayonnaise, then top with burgers, bacon mixture, and, if desired, lettuce and tomato.

4 servings

TIP: *Serve with Grilled Fries! Microwave all-purpose potatoes until tender, then cut into wedges and toss with **Lawry's® Seasoned Salt, Garlic Salt** and/or **Seasoned Pepper** and olive oil. Grill, turning once, until golden and tender.*

Mix & Match Grilled Chicken Sandwiches

10 Sandwiches you'll love! In 3 easy steps...

1. Pour Lawry's® Marinade over boneless, skinless chicken, then marinate in refrigerator 30 minutes. Discard Marinade.

2. Grill chicken, turning once, 10 minutes or until chicken is thoroughly cooked.

3. Assemble sandwiches and enjoy!

Dijon & Honey Chicken BLT Sandwich

The Sandwich...	The Marinade...	The Toppings...	The Bread...
Chicken Brie	**Lawry's® Dijon & Honey Marinade** or **Lawry's® Herb & Garlic Marinade**	Brie cheese, green leaf lettuce, tomato and a mixture of Marinade & mayonnaise	hamburger buns or sandwich rolls
BLT Chicken	**Lawry's® Louisiana Red Pepper Marinade** or **Lawry's® Dijon & Honey Marinade**	bacon, tomato, avocado, Romaine lettuce and a mixture of Marinade & mayonnaise	sandwich rolls or flour tortillas
Caesar	**Lawry's® Lemon Pepper Marinade** or **Lawry's® Italian Garlic Steak Marinade**	Romaine lettuce and a mixture of Marinade, mayonnaise and parmesan cheese	Italian bread (grilled, if desired)
Pineapple Chicken	**Lawry's® Teriyaki Marinade** or **Lawry's® Caribbean Jerk Marinade**	grilled pineapple and lettuce	hamburger buns
Californian	**Lawry's® Hawaiian Marinade** or **Lawry's® Teriyaki Marinade**	bean sprouts, green onions and avocado	whole wheat rolls
Chicken & Cheddar	**Lawry's® Steak & Chop Marinade** or **Lawry's® Mesquite Marinade**	grilled onions, bell peppers and cheddar cheese	sandwich rolls or Italian bread
Chicken Avocado	**Lawry's® Baja Chipotle Marinade** or **Lawry's® Havana Garlic Lime Marinade**	Swiss cheese and avocado	pumpernickel bread
Chicken Fajita	**Lawry's® Mexican Chile & Lime Marinade** or **Lawry's® Tequila Lime Marinade**	grilled bell peppers and onions, guacamole and pepper Jack cheese	sandwich rolls or flour tortillas
Western	**Lawry's® Baja Chipotle Marinade** or **Lawry's® Mesquite Marinade**	cheddar cheese, sautéed mushrooms, onions and bell peppers	hamburger buns or sandwich rolls
Italian Bruschetta	**Lawry's® Italian Garlic Steak Marinade** or **Lawry's® Herb & Garlic Marinade**	tomato, fresh mozzarella, roasted red peppers and fresh basil leaves	garlic bread or focaccia

Twice Grilled Chicken Fajitas

PREP TIME: 15 minutes **MARINATE TIME:** 30 minutes
COOK TIME: 15 minutes

- ½ **cup Lawry's® Tequila Lime Marinade With Lime Juice**
- 1 **lb. boneless, skinless chicken breasts**
- 2 **medium green, yellow and/or red bell peppers, halved and seeded**
- 1 **small red onion, sliced**
- 6 **(10-in.) burrito size flour tortillas**
- 1 **cup shredded cheddar cheese (about 4 oz.)**
- 4 **Tbsp. Lawry's® Sesame Ginger Marinade With Mandarin Orange Juice**

1. In large resealable plastic bag, pour Lawry's® Tequila Lime Marinade With Lime Juice over chicken and vegetables; turn to coat. Close bag and marinate in refrigerator 30 minutes.

2. Remove chicken and vegetables from Marinade, discarding Marinade. Grill, turning once, 10 minutes or until chicken is thoroughly cooked and vegetables are tender; thinly slice.

3. On tortillas, evenly spoon chicken and vegetables, then top with cheese. Fold over ends, then tightly roll. Brush edges of each tortilla with 1 tablespoon Lawry's® Sesame Ginger Marinade With Mandarin Orange Juice to seal. Grill fajitas, seam-side-down, 2 minutes or until golden. Brush tops with Marinade, then turn and cook 1 minute; repeat with remaining Marinade. Garnish, if desired, with sour cream and shredded lettuce.

6 servings

Cheesy Havana Shrimp Panini

PREP TIME: 20 minutes   **MARINATE TIME:** 30 minutes
COOK TIME: 10 minutes

- ¾ **cup PLUS 2 Tbsp. Lawry's® Havana Garlic & Lime Marinade With Lime Juice**
- 1½ **lbs. uncooked medium shrimp, peeled, deveined and tails removed**
- 1 **Tbsp. vegetable oil**
- 1½ **cups shredded Monterey Jack cheese (about 6 oz.)**
- ½ **cup Hellmann's® or Best Foods® Real Mayonnaise**
- ¼ **cup finely chopped red onion**
- ¼ **cup chopped fresh cilantro**
- 12 **slices crusty country white bread**
- 2 **Tbsp. Shedd's Spread Country Crock® Spread, melted**

1. In large resealable plastic bag, pour ¾ cup Lawry's® Havana Garlic & Lime Marinade With Lime Juice over shrimp; turn to coat. Close bag and marinate in refrigerator 30 minutes.

2. Remove shrimp from Marinade, discarding Marinade. In 12-inch nonstick skillet, heat oil over medium-high heat and cook shrimp, stirring occasionally, until shrimp turn pink. Drain; cool slightly, then coarsely chop.

3. Meanwhile, in large bowl, combine next 4 ingredients with remaining 2 tablespoons Marinade. Add shrimp and toss gently. On 6 bread slices, evenly spoon shrimp mixture, then top with remaining bread slice; brush outsides of sandwiches with Spread.

4. In panini grill, cook sandwiches 4 minutes or until golden brown.

6 servings

Grilled Garlic Bread Cheese Steaks

PREP TIME: 20 minutes   **MARINATE TIME:** 30 minutes
COOK TIME: 15 minutes

1	cup Lawry's® Steak & Chop Marinade With Garlic & Cracked Black Pepper
¾	lb. skirt steak or flank steak
¼	cup Shedd's Spread Country Crock® Spread, melted
½	tsp. Lawry's® Garlic Salt
1	loaf (about 16 oz.) French bread, halved lengthwise
1	medium onion, cut into ½-inch thick slices
3	small portobello mushrooms (about ⅓ lb.), stems removed and discarded
1	medium green bell pepper, quartered
1	cup shredded Monterey Jack cheese (about 4 oz.)

1. In large resealable plastic bag, pour ½ cup Lawry's® Steak & Chop Marinade With Garlic & Cracked Black Pepper over steak; turn to coat. Close bag and marinate in refrigerator 30 minutes.

2. Meanwhile, in small bowl, combine Spread with Lawry's® Garlic Salt. Evenly brush bread with Spread mixture, then grill.

3. Remove steak from Marinade, discarding Marinade. Grill steak and vegetables, turning once and brushing with remaining ½ cup Marinade, 15 minutes or until steak is desired doneness; remove. Slice steak and vegetables.

4. On bread, evenly arrange steak, vegetables and cheese, then cut into 4 sandwiches.

4 servings

*Also terrific with **Lawry's® Mexican Chile & Lime Marinade With Lime Juice.***

TIP: *For easier grilling, skewer onions.*

Tucson Chicken Wings with Blue Cheese Dipping Sauce

PREP TIME: 10 minutes   **MARINATE TIME:** 30 minutes
COOK TIME: 20 minutes

3 lbs. chicken drummettes or chicken wings, tips removed and cut in half at joint

1 cup Lawry's® Mexican Chile & Lime Marinade With Lime Juice

½ cup crumbled blue cheese

¼ cup Hellmann's® or Best Foods® Real Mayonnaise

¼ cup sour cream

1. In large resealable plastic bag, pour ½ cup Lawry's® Mexican Chile & Lime Marinade With Lime Juice over chicken. Close bag and marinate in refrigerator 30 minutes.

2. Meanwhile, in small bowl, combine blue cheese, Mayonnaise, sour cream and 1 tablespoon Marinade; set aside.

3. Remove chicken from Marinade, discarding Marinade. Grill chicken over medium heat, turning frequently and brushing with remaining ½ cup Marinade, 20 minutes until chicken is thoroughly cooked. Serve with Blue Cheese Dipping Sauce.

12 appetizer servings

*Also terrific with **Lawry's® Baja Chipotle Marinade With Lime Juice.***

Lawry's® Grilled Chicken Nachos

PREP TIME: 30 minutes   **MARINATE TIME:** 30 minutes
COOK TIME: 15 minutes

- ¾ **cup PLUS 2 Tbsp. Lawry's® Herb & Garlic Marinade With Lemon Juice**
- 1 **lb. boneless, skinless chicken breasts**
- 1 **medium onion, cut into ½-inch thick slices**
- 3 **medium tomatoes, chopped**
- 1 **serrano chili, seeded and finely chopped**
- ½ **tsp. Lawry's® Garlic Salt**
- ¼ **tsp. Lawry's® Seasoned Pepper**
- 1 **bag (11 oz.) plain tortilla chips**
- 2 **cups shredded cheddar or Monterey Jack cheese (about 8 oz.)**
- 1 **avocado, diced**
- 1 **Tbsp. lime juice**

1. In large resealable plastic bag, pour ½ cup Lawry's® Herb & Garlic Marinade With Lemon Juice over chicken and onion; turn to coat. Close bag and marinate in refrigerator 30 minutes.

2. Meanwhile, in medium bowl, combine tomatoes, chili, Lawry's® Garlic Salt and Lawry's® Seasoned Pepper; set aside.

3. Remove chicken and onion from Marinade, discarding Marinade. Grill chicken and onion, turning once and brushing with additional ¼ cup Marinade, 10 minutes or until chicken is thoroughly cooked and onion is tender. Shred chicken and chop onion.

4. In medium bowl, combine chicken, onion and remaining 2 tablespoons Marinade. In center of double layer (18×18-inch pieces) heavy-duty aluminum foil, arrange tortilla chips, then top with chicken mixture and cheese. Grill 1 minute or until cheese is melted. To serve, top with tomato mixture, drained if desired, avocado and lime juice.

6 servings

Sides, Veggies & Breads

Spicy Barbecued Corn

PREP TIME: 10 minutes   **MARINATE TIME:** 30 minutes
COOK TIME: 10 minutes

- ¾ cup Lawry's® Havana Garlic & Lime Marinade With Lime Juice*
- 6 ears fresh corn-on-the-cob
- 1½ tsp. Lawry's® Garlic Salt
- ½ tsp. dried chili flakes or 3 to 4 dried chili peppers, seeded and crumbled

1. In large resealable plastic bag, pour Lawry's® Havana Garlic & Lime Marinade With Lime Juice over corn; turn to coat. Close bag and marinate in refrigerator 30 minutes.

2. Remove corn from Marinade, discarding Marinade. Grill or broil corn, turning occasionally, 10 minutes or until tender.

3. Before serving, sprinkle corn with Lawry's® Garlic Salt and chili flakes.

6 servings

Also terrific with Lawry's® Tequila Lime Marinade With Lime Juice.

*SUBSTITUTION: *Use Lawry's® Louisiana Red Pepper Marinade With Lemon Juice and omit Lawry's® Havana Garlic & Lime Marinade With Lime Juice and chili flakes.*

Grilled Zucchini with Pine Nuts & Goat Cheese

PREP TIME: 5 minutes   **MARINATE TIME:** 30 minutes
COOK TIME: 6 minutes

- ½ **cup Lawry's® Lemon Pepper Marinade With Lemon Juice**
- 2 **lbs. zucchini, halved lengthwise**
- ½ **cup pine nuts, toasted**
- ½ **cup crumbled goat cheese**

1. In large resealable plastic bag, pour ¼ cup Lawry's® Lemon Pepper Marinade With Lemon Juice over zucchini; turn to coat. Close bag and marinate in refrigerator 30 minutes.

2. Remove zucchini from Marinade, discarding Marinade. Grill or broil zucchini, turning once and brushing frequently with remaining ¼ cup Marinade, 6 minutes or until tender; coarsely chop.

3. Toss zucchini with pine nuts, then top with cheese.

4 servings

*Also terrific with **Lawry's® Herb & Garlic Marinade With Lemon Juice** or **Lawry's® Italian Garlic Steak Marinade With Roasted Garlic & Olive Oil.***

Grilled Potato & Avocado Salad

PREP TIME: 20 minutes   **COOK TIME:** 35 minutes

1½	**lbs. all-purpose potatoes, cut into ½-inch chunks**
2	**medium red bell peppers, cut into ½-inch pieces**
1	**medium red onion, cut into ½-inch pieces**
½	**cup Lawry's® Italian Garlic Steak Marinade With Roasted Garlic & Olive Oil**
1	**tsp. Lawry's® Seasoned Salt**
1	**tsp. Lawry's® Seasoned Pepper**
¼	**cup Hellmann's® or Best Foods® Real Mayonnaise**
1	**medium avocado, diced**
2	**Tbsp. chopped fresh cilantro**

1. In large bowl, toss potatoes, vegetables, Lawry's® Italian Garlic Steak Marinade With Roasted Garlic & Olive Oil, Seasoned Salt and Seasoned Pepper.

2. In center of double layer (18×24-inch pieces) heavy-duty aluminum foil, arrange potato mixture. Wrap foil loosely around potatoes and vegetables, sealing edges airtight with double fold. Grill, turning occasionally, 45 minutes or until potatoes are tender; cool slightly.

3. In large bowl, toss potato mixture with Mayonnaise, then gently stir in avocado and cilantro. Serve warm or at room temperature.

6 servings

TIP: *For a complete meal, stir in 1 lb. shredded cooked chicken and serve, if desired, over salad greens.*

Grilled Ratatouille

PREP TIME: 10 minutes   **MARINATE TIME:** 30 minutes
COOK TIME: 12 minutes

1¼	cups Lawry's® Herb & Garlic Marinade With Lemon Juice
3	medium tomatoes, halved
1	medium zucchini, halved lengthwise
1	medium yellow squash, halved lengthwise
1	medium eggplant (about 1½ lbs.), cut into ¼-inch thick slices
1	large red onion, cut into ½-inch thick slices
4	ounces Parmigiano-Reggiano cheese, shaved

1. In 13×9-inch glass baking dish, combine Lawry's® Herb & Garlic Marinade With Lemon Juice with vegetables. Cover and marinate 30 minutes.

2. Remove vegetables from Marinade, reserving Marinade. Grill vegetables, turning occasionally and brushing frequently with reserved Marinade, 12 minutes or until tender; coarsely chop. Top with cheese. Serve, if desired, with hot cooked rice.

7 cups

Also terrific with **Lawry's® Italian Garlic Steak Marinade With Roasted Garlic & Olive Oil.**

TIP: *For easier grilling, skewer onions.*

Grilled Chicken & Veggie Macaroni Salad

PREP TIME: 15 minutes   **MARINATE TIME:** 30 minutes
COOK TIME: 20 minutes

½	cup Lawry's® Herb & Garlic Marinade With Lemon Juice
¾	lb. boneless, skinless chicken breast
1	medium sweet onion, cut into ½-inch slices
1	medium red bell pepper, quartered and seeded
2	stalks celery
1	cup Hellmann's® or Best Foods® Real Mayonnaise
2	Tbsp. white vinegar
1½	tsp. Lawry's® Seasoned Salt
1	tsp. sugar
½	tsp. Lawry's® Seasoned Pepper
8	ounces elbow macaroni, cooked, rinsed with cold water and drained

1. In separate large resealable plastic bags, pour ¼ cup Lawry's® Herb & Garlic Marinade With Lemon Juice over chicken and ¼ cup Marinade over vegetables; turn to coat. Close bag and marinate in refrigerator 30 minutes.

2. Remove chicken and vegetables from Marinade; discarding Marinade. Grill or broil chicken and vegetables, turning once, 10 minutes or until chicken is thoroughly cooked and vegetables are tender; cool slightly, then chop.

3. In large bowl, combine remaining ingredients except macaroni. Stir in macaroni, chicken and vegetables. Serve chilled or at room temperature.

8 servings

*Also terrific with any of your favorite **Lawry's® Marinades**.*

TIP: *For creamier salad, add additional Mayonnaise.*

Grilled Corn & Black-Eyed Pea Salad

PREP TIME: 15 minutes   **COOK TIME:** 8 minutes

3	Tbsp. Bertolli® Classico™ Olive Oil
1½	tsp. Lawry's® Seasoned Salt
4	ears corn-on-the-cob
1	can (15 oz.) black-eyed peas, rinsed and drained
1	medium tomato, chopped
2	green onions, finely chopped
1	medium jalapeño pepper, seeded and finely chopped
2	Tbsp. lime juice
½	tsp. Lawry's® Garlic Salt
	Hot pepper sauce to taste (optional)

1. In small bowl, combine 2 tablespoons Olive Oil with 1 teaspoon Lawry's® Seasoned Salt; evenly brush on corn. Grill, turning occasionally, 8 minutes or until browned; cool. With knife, remove kernels from cobs.

2. In medium bowl, combine corn with remaining Olive Oil, Lawry's® Seasoned Salt and remaining ingredients. Serve chilled or at room temperature.

8 servings

TIP: *Serve with tortilla chips for a tasty appetizer.*

LAWRY'S®

Out of the Box
Grilling

Grilled Corn & Chicken Soup

PREP TIME: 15 minutes   **COOK TIME:** 20 minutes

- 4   ears corn-on-the-cob, husks removed
- 2   poblano peppers, halved and seeded
- 1   medium onion, cut into ½-inch thick slices
- ½   cup Lawry's® Mesquite Marinade With Lime Juice
- 3   Tbsp. all-purpose flour
- 2   cans (14.5 oz. ea.) chicken broth
- 1½   cups milk
- 2   cups shredded cooked chicken

1. Grill vegetables, turning occasionally and brushing with Lawry's® Mesquite Marinade With Lime Juice, 10 minutes or until vegetables are golden brown and tender. Cool slightly, then cut corn from cob and chop peppers and onion; set aside.

2. In small bowl, whisk flour with ¼ cup broth; set aside.

3. In 4-quart saucepot, combine remaining broth, milk and vegetables. Bring to a boil over high heat, stirring occasionally. Stir in flour mixture. Bring to a boil over high heat, then reduce heat to medium-low and simmer, stirring occasionally, 5 minutes. Stir in chicken and cook 2 minutes or until heated through. Garnish, if desired, with cilantro, sour cream and lime wedges.

6 servings

Grilled Potato, Sausage & Pepper Breakfast

PREP TIME: 15 minutes   **COOK TIME:** 30 minutes

1	lb. red potatoes, cut into ½-inch pieces
2	medium red and/or yellow bell peppers, sliced
1	medium onion, sliced
1	tsp. Lawry's® Seasoned Salt
½	tsp. Lawry's® Garlic Salt
¼	tsp. Lawry's® Seasoned Pepper
8	ounces bulk Italian sausage, removed from casings and crumbled
½	cup shredded cheddar cheese (about 2 oz.)

1. In center of double layer (18×24-inch pieces) heavy-duty aluminum foil sprayed with nonstick cooking spray, arrange potatoes, peppers and onion. Sprinkle with Lawry's® Seasoned Salt, Garlic Salt and Seasoned Pepper, then top with sausage.

2. Wrap foil loosely around potato mixture, sealing edges airtight with double fold. Grill, turning occasionally, 30 minutes or until potatoes are tender and sausage is cooked.

3. Remove from grill, then sprinkle with cheese. Serve, if desired, with eggs and toast.

6 servings

Grilled Cake & Fruit with Spicy Raspberry & Sweet Velvet Sauces

PREP TIME: 15 minutes   **COOK TIME:** 5 minutes

½ **cup Shedd's Spread Country Crock® Spread, melted**

¼ **cup firmly packed brown sugar**

1 **tsp. Lawry's® Seasoned Salt**

1 **(12 oz.) prepared pound cake, cut into 8 slices (1-inch thick)**

3 **medium peaches, cut in half**

3 **medium banana, halved lengthwise**

6 **slices fresh pineapple**

Spicy Raspberry Sauce*

Sweet Velvet Sauce**

1. In medium bowl, combine Spread, brown sugar and Lawry's® Seasoned Salt. Evenly brush cake and fruit with Spread mixture.

2. Grill, turning once, 2 minutes or until cake is golden and fruit is tender. Remove and slice peaches in quarters, bananas and pineapple in half. Serve with Spicy Raspberry and Sweet Velvet sauces.

*For Spicy Raspberry Sauce, combine ¾ cup seedless raspberry preserves, ¼ teaspoon **Lawry's® Seasoned Salt** and ¼ to ½ teaspoon hot pepper sauce, then microwave on HIGH 30 seconds or until preserves are melted.*

For Sweet Velvet Sauce, combine 1 container (8 oz.) sour cream, ¼ cup brown sugar and ½ teaspoon **Lawry's® Seasoned Salt.*

8 servings

Breakfast Quesadillas

PREP TIME: 10 minutes   **COOK TIME:** 8 minutes

  4 **eggs, lightly beaten**
 ¼ **tsp. Lawry's® Seasoned Salt**
 ¼ **tsp. Lawry's® Seasoned Pepper**
  8 **(6-in.) fajita-size flour tortillas**
 ¼ **cup Lawry's® Herb & Garlic Marinade With Lemon
      Juice**
  2 **cups baby spinach leaves**
  1 **cup shredded mozzarella cheese (about 4 oz.)**
  1 **cup chopped tomato**

1. In 10-inch nonstick skillet sprayed with nonstick cooking spray, cook eggs with Lawry's® Seasoned Salt and Seasoned Pepper over medium heat, stirring frequently, 4 minutes or until done; set aside.

2. Brush 4 tortillas with Lawry's® Herb & Garlic Marinade With Lemon Juice. Evenly top tortillas with spinach, eggs, mozzarella and tomatoes; top with remaining tortillas.

3. On grill or in same skillet, cook quesadillas, turning once, 4 minutes or until cheese is melted. Cut quesadillas into wedges and serve, if desired, with sour cream.

4 servings

Grill's Night Off

Oven-Fried BBQ Glazed Chicken

PREP TIME: 10 minutes   **COOK TIME:** 40 minutes

- 1 **cup all-purpose flour**
- 1 **Tbsp. Lawry's® Seasoned Salt**
- 1 **tsp. Lawry's® Garlic Salt**
- 1 **tsp. Lawry's® Seasoned Pepper**
- 3 **lbs. chicken legs and/or bone-in chicken thighs**
- 1 **cup milk**
- 1 **cup barbecue sauce**

1. Preheat oven to 425°F. Spray jelly roll pan with nonstick cooking spray; set aside.

2. In large resealable plastic bag, combine flour, Lawry's® Seasoned Salt, Garlic Salt and Seasoned Pepper. Dip chicken in milk, then add to bag; shake to coat. On prepared pan, arrange chicken skin-side up.

3. Bake, turning once, 35 minutes. Generously coat with barbecue sauce. Bake an additional 5 minutes or until chicken is thoroughly cooked.

8 servings

Slow Cooked Ropa Vieja

PREP TIME: 15 minutes   **COOK TIME:** 4 hours

- 1   **can (14.5 oz.) diced tomatoes, drained**
- ½   **cup Lawry's® Baja Chipotle Marinade With Lime Juice**
- 1   **medium green bell pepper, sliced**
- 1   **small onion, sliced**
- ½   **tsp. Lawry's® Seasoned Salt**
- 2   **lbs. flank steak, halved**
- **Hamburger buns**

1. In 3½- to 4-quart slow cooker, combine all ingredients except steak. Add steak; turn to coat.

2. Cook covered on HIGH 4 to 6 hours or LOW 8 to 10 hours. Remove steak.

3. With two forks, shred steak, then return to slow cooker; stir. Serve in buns.

6 servings

*Also terrific with **Lawry's® Mexican Chile & Lime Marinade With Lime Juice.***

VARIATION: *For Ropa Vieja Tacos, serve in flour tortillas with sour cream, shredded lettuce and cheese.*

Pulled Chicken on Corn Cakes

PREP TIME: 20 minutes   **COOK TIME:** 20 minutes

Chicken

- ½ **cup Lawry's® Mesquite Marinade With Lime Juice**
- ¼ **cup ketchup**
- 3 **Tbsp. firmly packed brown sugar**
- ½ **tsp. Lawry's® Seasoned Salt**
- 1 **cooked rotisserie chicken, meat pulled off the bone and shredded**

Cakes

- 1 **cup all-purpose flour**
- 1 **cup cornmeal**
- 2 **tsp. Lawry's® Seasoned Salt**
- ½ **tsp. baking powder**
- ¾ **cup buttermilk**
- ½ **cup water**
- ¼ **cup PLUS 4 Tbsp. vegetable oil**
- 2 **eggs, slightly beaten**

1. For Chicken, in 2-quart saucepan, combine all ingredients except chicken. Bring to a boil over high heat. Reduce heat to low and simmer 5 minutes. Stir in chicken and heat through; set aside and keep warm.

2. Meanwhile, for Cakes, in large bowl, mix first 4 ingredients. Stir in buttermilk, water, ¼ cup oil and eggs just until combined. In 12-inch nonstick skillet, heat 1 tablespoon oil over medium heat and drop cake mixture by 2 tablespoonfuls into skillet. Cook 4 minutes, turning once, or until golden brown; drain on paper towels. Repeat with remaining oil and cake mixture. Serve chicken on corn cakes.

8 servings

Cashew Chicken Stir Fry

PREP TIME: 15 minutes **MARINATE TIME:** 30 minutes
COOK TIME: 10 minutes

- ¼ **cup PLUS 2 Tbsp. Lawry's® Teriyaki Marinade With Pineapple Juice**
- 1 **lb. boneless, skinless chicken breast halves, cut into strips**
- 2 **Tbsp. vegetable oil**
- 3 **cups sliced assorted fresh vegetables (onion, bell peppers, carrots, snow peas and/or green beans)**
- 1 **cup chicken broth**
- 1 **Tbsp. cornstarch**
- ½ **to 1 cup salted cashews, toasted, if desired**

1. In large resealable plastic bag, pour ¼ cup Lawry's® Teriyaki Marinade With Pineapple Juice over chicken; turn to coat. Close bag and marinate in refrigerator 30 minutes.

2. In 12-inch nonstick skillet, heat 1 tablespoon oil over medium-high heat and cook chicken with Marinade, stirring occasionally, 5 minutes or until chicken is thoroughly cooked. Remove chicken from skillet; keep warm.

3. In same skillet, heat remaining 1 tablespoon oil and cook vegetables, stirring occasionally, until almost tender. Stir in remaining 2 tablespoons Marinade, broth and cornstarch. Bring to a boil over high heat. Reduce heat to low and simmer until sauce thickens. Return chicken to skillet and heat through; stir in cashews. Serve, if desired, over hot cooked rice.

4 servings

*Also terrific with **Lawry's® Sesame Ginger Marinade With Mandarin Orange Juice.***

Steak House Fajitas

PREP TIME: 10 minutes   **COOK TIME:** 10 minutes

2	tsp. vegetable oil
1	lb. boneless sirloin steak, cut into thin strips
1	medium green, red, yellow or orange bell pepper, cut into thin strips
½	medium red onion, thinly sliced
½	cup Lawry's® Steak & Chop Marinade With Garlic & Cracked Black Pepper
8	(6-in.) fajita size flour tortillas, warmed

1. In 12-inch nonstick skillet, heat oil over medium-high heat and brown steak. Add green pepper and onion. Cook, stirring occasionally, 3 minutes.

2. Stir in Lawry's® Steak & Chop Marinade With Garlic & Cracked Black Pepper. Cook, stirring occasionally, 5 minutes or until vegetables are crisp-tender. Serve in tortillas and, if desired, with sour cream, cheddar cheese and salsa.

4 servings

Also terrific with **Lawry's® Mesquite Marinade With Lime Juice.**

TIP: *For a Steak House Fajita Sub, instead of serving in tortillas, serve on 6-inch sandwich rolls and top with shredded cheddar or Monterey Jack cheese.*

Index